*rejoice
I
am*
you

poetry by arif gowani

Copyright © 2019 Arif Gowani

All rights reserved.

ISBN-13: 978-0-578-44381-2

Table of Contents

Introduction: 1

I 2
   rejoice I am you 3
   the Ink 5

us 7
   countless circles of love 8

universe(s) and nature 10
   at night 11
   My canvas 13
   feel the hugs of light 14
   rain drops 16
   each breath 17
   breeze 18
   flower 19
   leaves 21
   birds 22
   a tree 24

heart 25
   dust 26
   echo 28
   submit 29
   prostrate 30
   always with you 31
   attachments 32
   My real house 34

the Divine 35
   My Reflection and Spark 36
   My Grace 37
   Most High 38

your soul 39
   seek Me 40
   desires 41
   wings 42

- *sleep* 44
- **be mindful** 45
  - *ego* 46
  - *be aware* 47
  - *be humble* 48
  - *be wise* 50
- **pluralism** 51
  - *love all* 52
  - *strands* 53
  - *diversity* 55
  - *Oneness* 56
- **life** 57
  - *miracles* 58
  - *a clock* 59
  - *precious time* 60
  - *trials and tribulations* 61
  - *be good* 62
  - *be on guard* 63
  - *hope* 64
  - *stand up* 65
  - *blessings* 67
  - *in the end* 68
- **About Author/Poet:** 70

Introduction:

Poetry book focuses on self-realization of the inner strengths of oneself and of the Divine.

This poetry is written in such a way, that each reader will feel the direct conversation with the Divine.

To be touched and to feel the joy, you must read this poetry with an open heart and welcome inside the Divine Love.
The Divine you know and believe in, will be your own Guide.

To Get Notification for
New Releases by this Author/Poet:

Send Email directly to Author/Poet:

In **Subject** section please write: **Please Register My Email**

Author/Poet's email address:

arifgowani@gmail.com

I

rejoice I am you

I am your Lord
My Kingdom stretches above
all knowledge
all grounds and
over all universe(s)

I am
the only King

all that exist
is My Greatness

       let Me unveil
          Myself
             to you

listen to
My whisper

        rejoice
         I
        am
          you

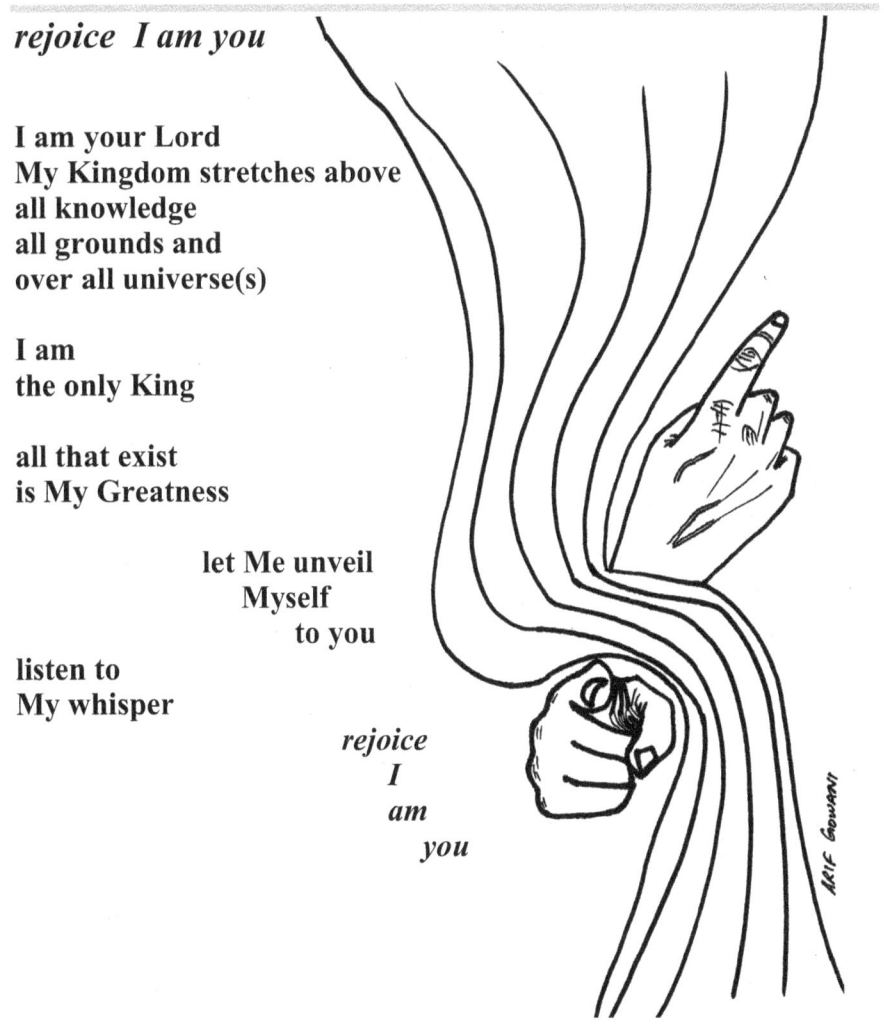

**your heart is
My Heart**

**experience
My Divine Presence
within you**

rejoice I am you - **arif gowani**

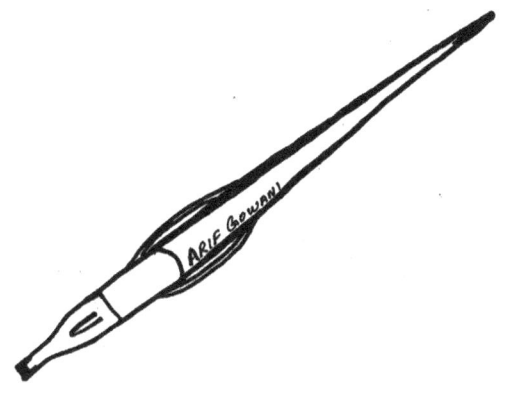

the Ink

a pen
named arif

through which
Divine's Ink flows

the Lord is
the Inscriber
the Beholder of this pen
yet He is invisible

as this Ink flows
the hidden secrets
intertwine twist like locks over each word
locks upon locks
veils upon veils
over each layer

then dried off
sealed off
with His Gentle Breath

His Will is
the only key
of wisdom

and is only given
to those
He chooses

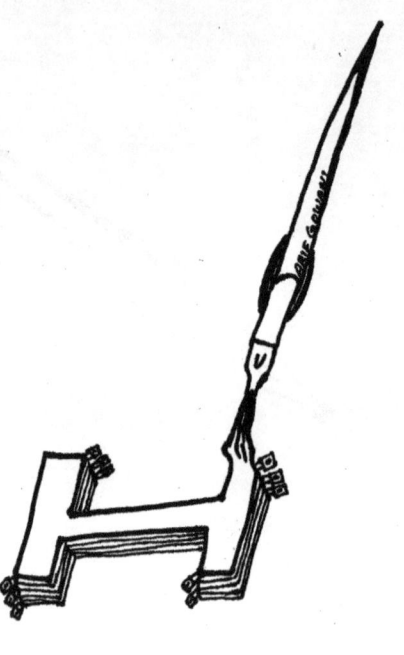

by
His Mercy and Grace
each secret is
unlocked
pealed off
unveiled
one by one

until the final veil
is lifted apart
between you and Him
blessed are you
now
see and feel
the Divine

the Ink - **arif gowani**

us

countless circles of love

not a sufi
a mystic or a sheikh
if you must know
arif does not dance or spin in love
but in reality
all that exists in all universe(s)
willingly and unwillingly are in motion within this rhythm
all together twisting spinning in
countless circles of love for the Divine
all chaos noise speed motion and spinning is occurring outside of
you so hold tight and do not get swept up by these
outside circles
all of us
are spinning in this ecstasy with universe(s)
yet there is no dizziness
because our hearts are at still

listen to arif
your heart must submit itself in
Remembrance of the Divine
countless spins of repetitions
twirling
inside the circles of Love
a rhythm of Divine Love
will take a shape of
a twister

a powerful force and
the gravity of Divine Love
will rip and pull
you apart
from you rself

you will no longer exist
now only remains
the <u>Real</u> <u>Self</u>
the Truth
your Lord

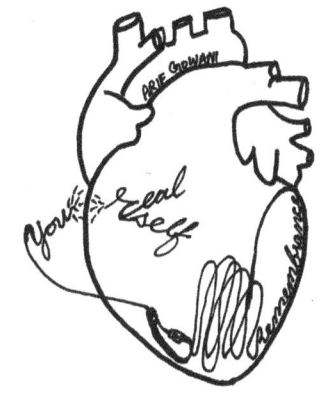

countless circles of love - **arif gowani**

universe(s) and nature

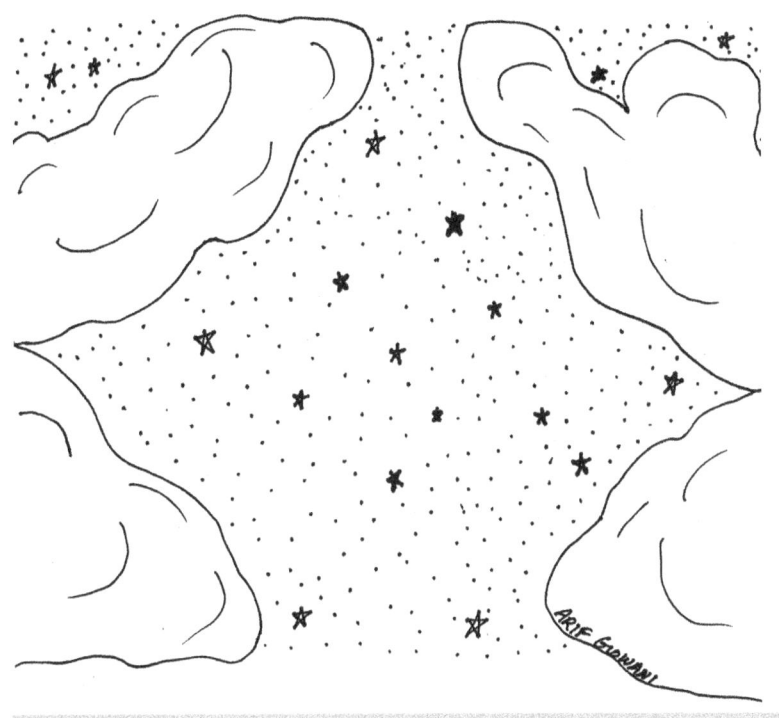

at night

I am
the stars
their dusts
their blinks and
their flashes
I am
the darkness
that exists behind the stars
I am
the clouds
which drapes over the night sky

at night
I am
the moon
which forces all the tides to rise up high
all praising My Greatness
in the seas
in the oceans
a sign for the mindful
at night
prostrate downwards
as the waves inside you
level down with humility
with hands open
submit yourself
all in praise of Me

at night - **arif gowani**

My canvas

universe(s)
in its entirety is
My canvas
on which
I display My Love
colors and shapes
so you may ponder
upon My canvas

everyday
I surround and cover
you with My Beauty

My beloved
you are
My masterpiece
My centerpiece
My Love

My canvas - **arif gowani**

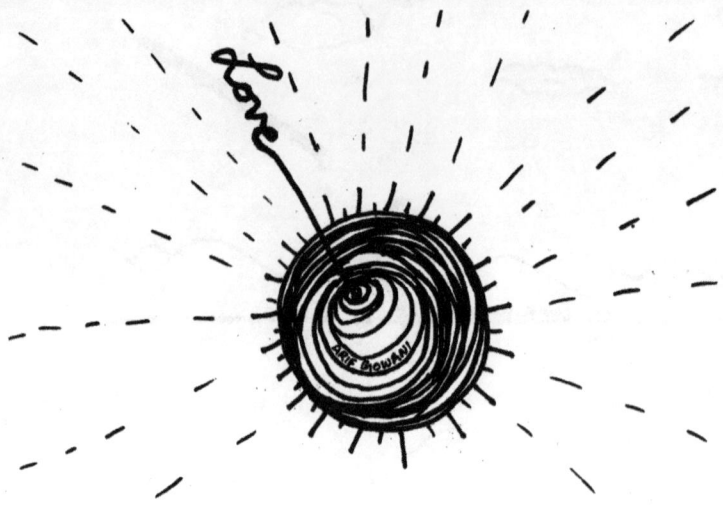

feel the hugs of light

just for My beloved
inside the sun

My Love
churns burns boils
just enough
to emit rays of light

as My Love falls
upon your skin

My Love filters
all rays to become
warm and gentle

as My Arms of rays
wrap around you
everyday
only
hugs
for My beloved
feel the hugs of light

feel the hugs of light - **arif gowani**

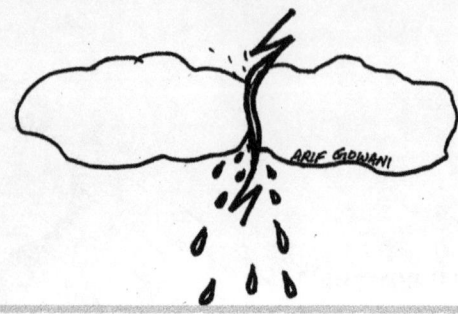

rain drops

that moment
when separation
overwhelms Me
clouds collide
hear the sound of thunder
My Love takes
a new identity
a new form

shape of tears

they burst
out as droplets
from the hearts of the sky
all falling down towards you

physically displaying
a sign
an evidence of
My Tears
for My Love
o beloved
My Heart misses you
look at these rain drops

rain drops **- arif gowani**

each breath

gently I placed
My Breath
over this earth
then ordained
plants forests and all vegetation to maintain
My Breath
only for you
My beloved

so may you have an ease
on every breathe

indeed
this is one of My favor

a reminder
of My blessing

inhale each breathe
with gratitude

each breath - **arif gowani**

breeze

**even though
you may not see Me**

**I kiss your cheeks
softly and gently
with
a breeze**

**reaffirming
My Love for you
everyday**

so reflect

breeze **- arif gowani**

flower

look at all the variations and colors
of
flowers

I placed over them
My beauty
to distract you
but still you
ignore

come close

behold My Beauty
inhale My Presence
open your heart

let this
Divine Fragrance of love
enter
in your heart
My beloved
I am
still waiting

flower - **arif gowani**

leaves

My love
as you travel
on land
just for your
heart's attention
I brush My fingers
over trees

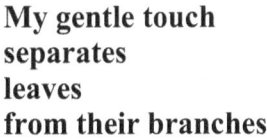

My gentle touch
separates
leaves
from their branches

slowly
gently
they swing
and fall downwards
before you

a welcome sign

of My shower of blessings
and of My affection

for your soul

leaves - **arif gowani**

birds

look at
birds
examples for you
in their
flight
shapes
sounds
beauty

as they fly
high up in the air
their hands are raised
and their wings are lifted

their flight
a sign of praise for
the Most High

at rest
on branches
each sing
its unique
musical note
of the Divine

their calls and
their praise are
also a reminder
for your soul

recite and praise
your Lord

birds - arif gowani

a tree

canopy of leaves
for shelter

palms of hands
for nest

thin fingers
rest stop for birds

fruits
for consumption

purified air
for living

a tree
is a spine
for all life existence
on this
earth

a tree - **arif gowani**

heart

dust

a dessert storm
clouds of dust
no visibility

arrogance
ignorance and
temptations
these layers of dust
lay over your heart
everyday

slowly
as these layers of dust solidifies

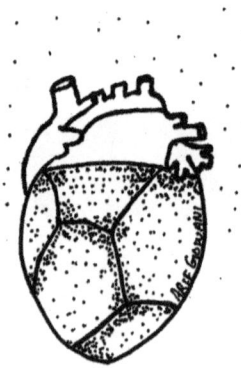

a rock forms
around your heart

no feelings
no caring
no humanity
no understanding

slowly blindness and
deafness takes over
ultimately
there is complete darkness

still there is hope and a cure
for your heart
believe Me
and
call upon your Lord's Name
with a pure heart
slowly
warmth of My Name
will crack open
this rock
like an egg
then
thick molten lava
will gush and slowly
flow through
all the dirt and the layers of dust
until your heart grounds become
soft as a fertile land
then
My Mercy
will take control
and will blossom
fresh new roses
on the grounds of your heart
their Fragrance
will be the confirmation of
My Presence
rejoice

dust - **arif gowani**

echo

with a silent tongue
inside
call upon the Name of your Lord

listen carefully
you will hear
an echo
from your heart
this can
only occur when
your Heart becomes hollow
let go of all the attachments

echo - **arif gowani**

submit

I do not desire
your tears that fall on your cheeks
your wealth or
your gifts

I desire only your heart

submit
your heart
your own self
to Me

tears awaits
your heart
once the realization
of separation
from your Lord
is felt

hot tears
will gush
boil
and burst out
like hot springs
from your heart

surely this will
purify your soul

submit - **arif gowani**

prostrate

animals hit their faces
towards the ground
thousands of times

just as you prostrate your face
during prayers
only few times

evaluate the difference

do one favor
to your own soul

prostrate along with your heart

I
your Lord
wish only
your heart

prostrate - **arif gowani**

always with you

blanket of
stars and it dust

the vastness of the sky
all visible universe

all can inset
at once
in your small eyes

verily
believe
I
My Greatness
My Love
My Light
can also
confine itself
in your heart

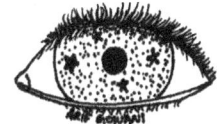

your heart is My Castle
My Throne is set here
not above in the sky

o beloved
from now onwards
seek Me inwards
I assure you that
I am always with you

always with you - **arif gowani**

attachments

do not attach
your heart
to this world

all that you see will perish

this is life

tame your heart in a manner
to break and
loosen all these
worldly chains
of attachments

so when your time comes
for the separation
that moment
there will be
no struggle
no pain
of detachment

attachments - **arif gowani**

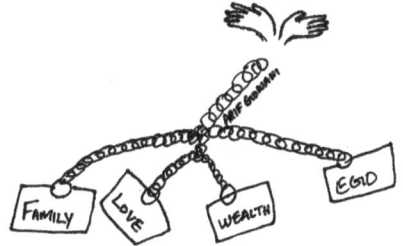

My real house

church
mosque
temple
and other
house of prayers
carry sounds of
praises within their walls

o beloved
but My real house
is in your heart
listen to these walls
of silence
these walls also need My praise
call upon My Divine Name
until your heart walls
can echo
and emit
My Attributes
through your personality

My real house – **arif gowani**

the Divine

My Reflection and Spark

give a smile
to an infant
in response
you will receive
a pure and genuine
smile
indeed
this is My Reflection

now gaze into their
sparkly
shiny
crystal
clear eyes
they behold My Brightness
My Spark

seek to
experience
My Reflection and Spark

I kindle and dwell in All

My Reflection and Spark **- arif gowani**

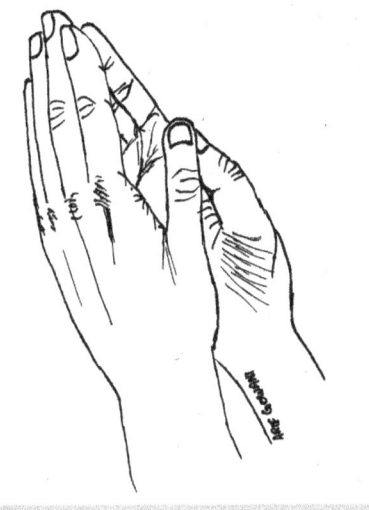

My Grace

**all good you
see
feel and
experience
are all
My Blessings**

My beloved

**be thankful
be grateful**

all is My Grace

My Grace - **arif gowani**

Most High

do not limit Me
with your minds and tongues

your words cannot
capture My Greatness

before
creation

only
I
existed

I am
omniscient
omnipresent
omnipotent

I am the First and the Last
Beginning and the End

I am Above all
and the Most High

Most High - **arif gowani**

your soul

seek Me

o beloved
you must
seek Me

everyday
slowly
I reveal
to you
Myself and
the secrets
of universe(s)

your soul
desires only
Me
this is the Truth
seek Me

seek Me - **arif gowani**

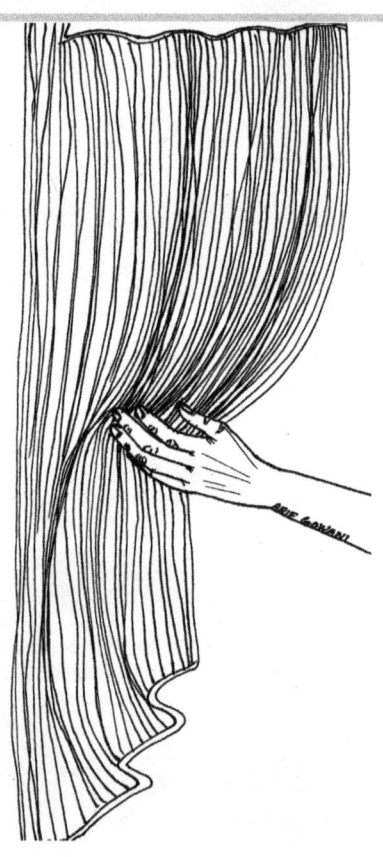

11:11 PM

desires

every moment
your heart desires
worldly temptations
but
your soul desires
only
the closeness
with the Lord

balance both desires
between material and spiritual progress
because
time is
very limited and
is irreversible

desires - **arif gowani**

wings

you tie strings of attachments
with weights of
ego
temptations
anger
lust
pride
greed
and
hate
to your wings

even if you wish
to fly
unable to do so

these weights will keep
your Soul down

you must
cut off theses weighty
strings of attachments

your inside
must become hollow
and light hearted

experience
this Truth of detachment

practice
to flap your wings
with
the beats
of the Divine music

the music of Remembrance

your soul belongs high with Me
I am your destiny
put your trust and faith in Me
I will enable you
to fly
soar high towards Me
take a plunge
I will hold you
against all gravity

until We Reunite
you are My beloved

wings - arif gowani

sleep

until the moment you fall asleep
you are busy in worldly matters

this is why
I come after you fall asleep
in the middle of the night

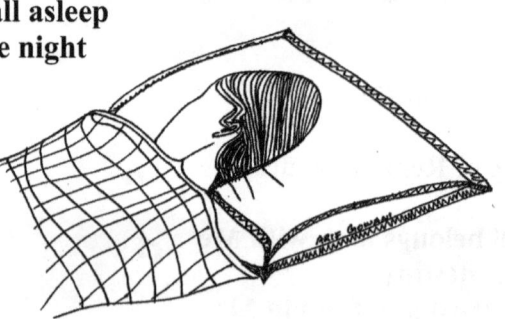

I wake you up
by means above
your intellect

but everyday
you choose sleep
over My Presence

sole reason for My arrival
is to
convey
console
and bless
your soul
individually

I will come again
tonight

sleep – **arif gowani**

be mindful

ego

do not puff with pride
on your
achievements and
accomplishments

the truth is
everything
was and is
My Blessings

I reveal slowly
as I will
I am the Source
of all intellect
and
the Truth of knowledge itself
from the Beginning
till the End

be humble
respect and accept
your Lord's Greatness

your ego must not exist
in My Presence

be grateful and be humble

ego - arif gowani

be aware

be aware
be in control

do not let the evil enter
through the doors of your thoughts
and make you slip
from the right path

be cautious
in every move

keep yourself away from sins
so in the end
no need for
your soul to repent

be aware - **arif gowani**

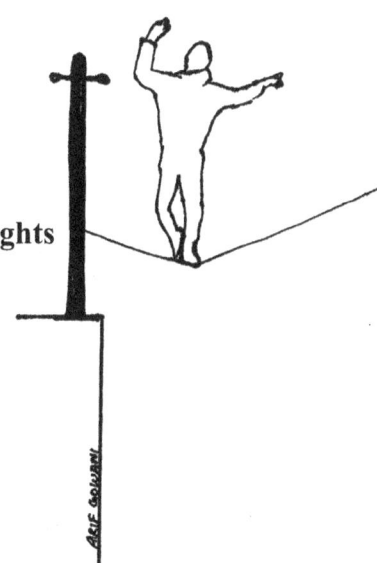

be humble

rigid
trees

its trunk
their spine

its branches
their arms

leaves
their skin

its fruits
for gratitude

all prostrate
downwards

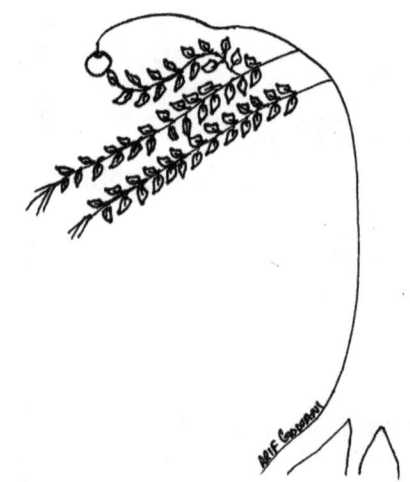

everything that exists

prostrates for the Divine
willingly and unwillingly

observe
their shadows
as they move from
right to left

a symbol of
complete
submission

contemplate

do not be rigid with ego

your inner spine
must submit

be humble

be humble - **arif gowani**

be wise

allocated
a fixed time
for you
on this earth

by My permission
you are granted
a free will

so be wise
in your choices

I know
the destiny

of all your decisions

be wise - **arif gowani**

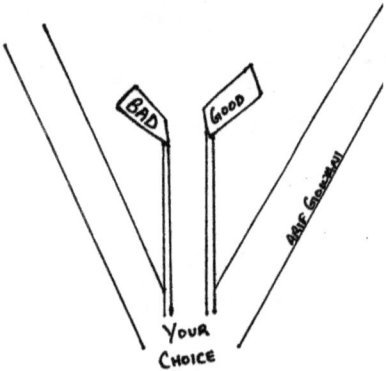

pluralism

love all

**My Will
created
diversity
among all people
so that you may
respect
learn
experience
and share
amongst each other
diversity is indeed a strength**

**wise amongst you
will accept
My Will
and will love all**

love all - **arif gowani**

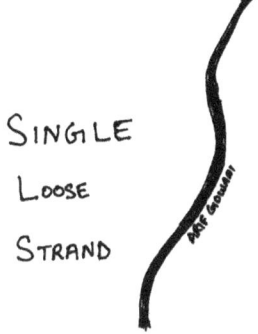

strands

**you
a single loose strand**

weak by yourself

you must
connect
intertwine
interlace
interlock
with other strands
to become

one strong fabric
one humanity
this is pluralism

strands - **arif gowani**

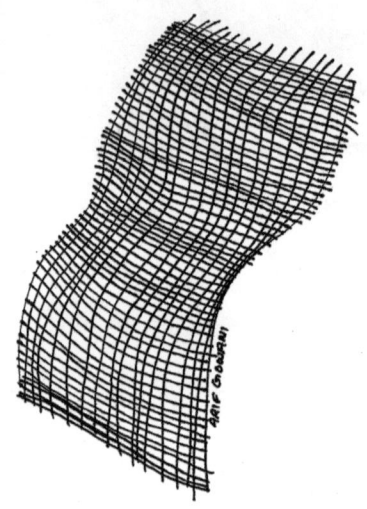

diversity

flowers
all are different and beautiful

if gathered together
then will display
My beauty in diversity

same
I have spread among
all mankind

you are My flower

each one of you behold
My beauty

feel My Attribute
in diversity

I am hidden
in the fragrance

diversity - **arif gowani**

Oneness

the fuels of
your own ego

you insert
seeds of
fear
hate and
divisions
amongst people's hearts

Lord's religion is
only peace love and unity

indeed
all mankind was created from
a Single Soul

a reason
to love one another

a common relationship
between all souls

lift this veil
and
see the Oneness

Oneness - **arif gowani**

life

miracles

in darkness
many months
upside down
inside your mother's womb

I provided for you
all the essentials
My miracle

I kept you alive without
burdening your lungs
My miracle

only for you
I turned blood into milk
before you were born
My miracle

so how many of My Favors you will deny

miracles - **arif gowani**

a clock

when you go to
a funeral
of a stranger
or of a loved one

a reminder
a notification
awaits you

for your soul

of which
limits were set
for the appointed term

a clock
with a precise measure
that ticks your life
with each breathe

a clock - arif gowani

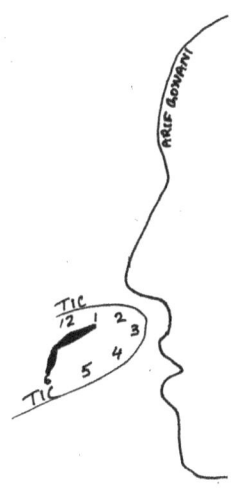

precious time

all the wealth in this world
cannot reverse time

time is
very precious
and valuable

take joy in this
present moment

appreciate
all the blessings
and unite hearts
before they vanish

precious time - **arif gowani**

trials and tribulations

when you pass through
the veil
of trials and tribulations

that moment in time

you must
seek strength
from your Lord
to endure all
you must overcome

all you experience
feel and
see
is finite and
is temporary

truth of the matter is that
when you beseech from your Lord
at those very moments
spiritually
your soul gets more
and more closer to the Divine

always remember behind
the veil of darkness
awaits for you brightness
in the end
only Light shall remain

trials and tribulations - **arif gowani**

be good

do not
compare
and
be astonished by
their children
their wealth and
their luxuries
of those who choose the
sinful paths
truth of this matter is
that
I
your Lord
gives them more time
so they may increase their sins
but
you
My dear
are My favorite
one wrongful act and
you will address
consequences
because
I will restrain you now
so later
your soul may experience only peace
verily
enormous reward awaits your soul
you are My beloved
so be good

be good - **arif gowani**

be on guard

strangers friends and family
all cross your path

only handful of those
are genuine

but
some have evil intentions
of hurting your feelings

and some just want to
provoke anger

this is the enjoyment
they seek
in this manner slowly
evil's ill will takes over their minds

be on guard
practice patience

be on guard - **arif gowani**

hope

roller coaster of life
you struggle and work hard
to reach
a goal
a height
which gets
higher and higher
as time passes
sometimes
tracks of life
curve downwards
that moment
you only see and feel
fear

remember
deep inside of you
there is
a hidden force
which will help
you to rebound
back up again
even after the fall

hope
is that dynamic force
which will push
you forward and upwards
until you propel

lean on hope

hope – **arif gowani**

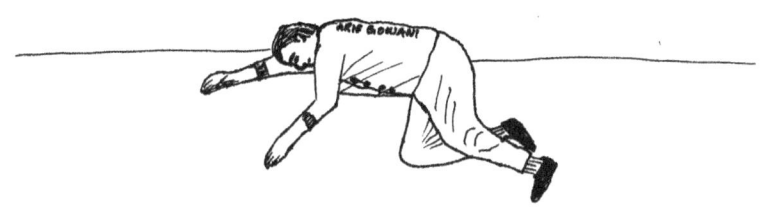

stand up

loss of
health
lives
wealth and
other matters
will force you to
fall down

in life
several times
you will fall
but your will
your strong desire
to stand up and
to keep moving forward
will overshadow
these rough times

this is life

seek strength and courage
from your Lord

always have hope
to overcome

this shall also pass
verily
blessings are written in your destiny
have faith

stand up - **arif gowani**

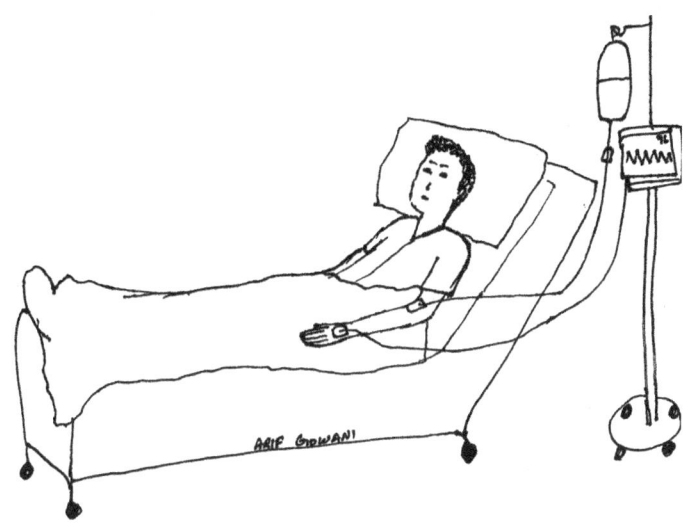

blessings

the value of good
health
family
friends
and life
is not appreciated
until
it is too late
or
when it is lost

giving respect later
does not make sense

cherish and
respect each now

all are My blessings

blessings - **arif gowani**

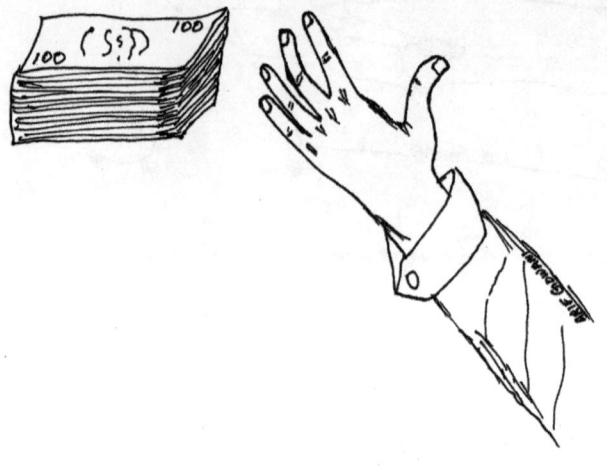

in the end

desires
to snatch others
wealth
power
respect
happiness
peace
friends
families

this is
an animal instinct

be human
do not be an animal

remember
in the end
DEATH
snatches
all that you have gathered

in the end – **arif gowani**

About Author/Poet:

Arif Gowani is an Author, Poet and Artist. Since childhood he loved art and throughout his life has created many artworks. One common issue that he noticed in all the art exhibitions was that there was very limited option to write the complete details of artist intentions or perspective.
In 2018, Arif Gowani started a new journey in the world of poetry. This journey has opened new opportunities for author's art illustrations to display along with poems.
The Author/Poet is not and does not claim to be as a Sufi, Mystic, Sheikh, Guru, Monk or any other high-ranking individual.
The Author/Poet was born in Karachi, Pakistan and now resides in Grand Prairie, Texas.

To Get Notification for New Releases by this Author/Poet:

Send Email directly to Author/Poet:
In <u>Subject</u> section please write: <u>Please Register My Email</u>

Author/Poet's email address:
arifgowani@gmail.com

www.ingramcontent.com/pod-product-compliance
Lightning Source LLC
Chambersburg PA
CBHW022121090426
42743CB00008B/944